why me?
humiliationHOTsheet

EDITED BY APRYL LUNDSTEN

ILLUSTRATED BY MONICA GESUE

Scholastic Inc.

New York Toronto London Auckland Sydney
Mexico City New Delhi Hong Kong

0-439-11469-1

Distributed under license from
The Petersen Publishing Company, L.L.C.
Copyright © 2001 The Petersen Publishing
Company, L.L.C. All rights reserved.
Published by Scholastic Inc.

 Produced by 17th Street Productions,
an Alloy Online, Inc. company
33 West 17th Street
New York, NY 10011

Teen and why me? are trademarks
of Petersen Publishing Company, L.L.C.

12 11 10 9 8 7 6 5 4   4 5 6/0

Printed in the U.S.A.
First Scholastic printing, June 2001

This book is dedicated to all the girls who've blown it in front of a cutie, made fools of yourselves in class, messed up around the in-crowd, or been humiliated by an obnoxious sib. Especially my cousin Jenna.

INTRODUCTION

By some wacky twist of cosmic universal fate, we are all subject to serious humiliation at one time or another. (Some of us just suffer through it more times than we'd like to admit!)

Whether you've blown it while trying to impress your crush, in front of the whole school, or just hanging out with your buds, chances are you've embarrassed yourself somehow! But that's okay because one thing's for sure—mortifying moments happen to everyone.

Believe it or not, even your favorite celeb has had a humiliating experience or two. *Dharma & Greg* star Jenna Elfman had a serious overbite that won her the nickname Bucky Beaver in high school. And No Doubt songstress Gwen Stefani was caught "blue-handed" backstage at a concert when someone snapped a picture of the star readjusting her turquoise bikini!

At the time, the whole school seeing you in your undies can make you want to pack your bags and never show your face there again. But remember, even though your "performance" may never be forgotten, you can bet someone else will soon come along and take that "Most Embarrassed" title from you. And someday you'll probably be able to look back at the whole situation and crack up about how funny it was (now that it's over!).

Reading these stories will give you absolute proof that no matter how bad you think your situation was, there are many worse ones out there! Maybe you'll even discover that someone else faced the same humiliation you did. Just remember—everyone in here lived to tell about their embarrassing moments, and you will, too!

Chapter One:
Crush Crashes

Who's the last person on earth you would want to witness your supreme embarrassment? Yeah, we know—your crush. What could be worse than trying to impress the homeroom hottie but totally blowing it instead?

Fifteen-year-old Diana from Colorado knows exactly how it feels. You won't believe what she does in front of her sweetie—and how she gets snagged in the act!

Check out these crush crashes and see where yours fit in.

THE MORT-O-METER

"Heartly" Humiliating

Highly Humiliating

Horrifically Humiliating

I had *finally* scored a date with a total hottie that I'd been crushing on forever. The only problem was that I was barely allowed to talk on the phone with guys, let alone go to the movies with them! I told my mom that I was going out with my friend Dana. My date picked me up (my parents were out to dinner at the time), and we drove to the movie theater. It was an awkward car ride—we didn't have much to say to each other. But it was obvious there was some serious chemistry going on. All through the movie we kept almost touching—barely rubbing shoulders, hands, knees. After the movie ended, I had a half hour before I needed to be home, so we cruised around, finally flirting for real. When he pulled up in front of my house, he killed the engine and turned toward me. I was thinking, Oh my God, he's going to kiss me! I closed my eyes in anticipation. Instead of a kiss, though, the car door opened. It was my mom! She made both of us come inside, and my date got a huge lecture. Apparently Dana called while I was gone and blew my cover. Needless to say, I've never been out with him again!

Lana, 14, California

When my first boyfriend (of a month and a half!) broke up with me, I was really upset, but I didn't want him to know that. One night I came up with a great plan to show him I was over him. I called his house, and as soon as the phone picked up, I blasted the classic song "I Will Survive." When the song was over, I heard his mom saying, "Hello? Who is this?" I hung up right away. I couldn't believe my ex hadn't even answered the phone!

Val, 15, Colorado

EDITOR'S NOTE: MAKE SURE THE PERSON YOU'RE PRANKING ANSWERS THE PHONE BEFORE YOU START IN ON HIM!

My boyfriend was out of town for the weekend, so I went to a party with my best friend. The party was pretty lame, and we were thinking about leaving, but then I met this really snacky senior from our rival high school. We hit it off and ended up talking forever. My friend got bored and left after we decided that the guy would take me home. Once we got in his car, we started kissing like crazy. We made out until my curfew, then said good-bye and went our separate ways. I know it's terrible that I cheated, but I didn't feel very guilty. I went to bed thinking I had this great secret that no one knew about. The next morning when I went to take a shower, I caught a glimpse of myself in the mirror—I had a huge hickey on my neck! I wore a turtleneck for a whole week—during a major heat wave—and every time my boyfriend asked me why I was wearing that stupid hot shirt, my face would turn bright red. I told him I had a rash.

Kali, 16, Florida

EDITOR'S NOTE: TSK, TSK, KALI!

I was at a fair with my dad, and I was getting a little hungry. I was so engrossed in checking out this amazing-looking guy that I just reached into my dad's coat pocket, pulled out his wallet, and walked over to the hot dog stand. I ordered a deluxe dog with extra relish and went to pay for it. But when I opened my dad's wallet, I realized it wasn't his. I'd reached into some strange man's coat and taken his wallet! Even worse—it turned out to be my cutie's dad!

Deb, 14, Delaware

FIVE STEPS TO CRUSH CRASH DAMAGE CONTROL

FIRST, realize that he's most likely messed up in front of his crush before, too.

SECOND, laugh at yourself. Make him think that you're totally comfortable with your klutzy side—even if you're not.

THIRD, follow up your embarrassing moment with a memorable one. If you just totally blew it in front of him, stand up straight and look him in the eye. Maybe now's the time to say something like, "Wow! You're even cuter in person!" It will take his mind off what just happened, and he'll be psyched that you think he's cute.

FOURTH, if you've really just completely humiliated yourself, walk away with as much dignity as possible and try to keep a low profile for the next couple of days.

FIFTH, remember that eventually he'll forget all about it!

My mom is good friends with my crush's mom. After she overheard me telling someone how much I like him, she told her friend! I guess she thought maybe it would help me score him or something. Instead my crush's mom must have given him the information, and then he complained to all his friends that his mom was trying to set him up. Everyone thought I was so pathetic!

Steffani, 13, New Jersey

My best friend, Rachel, and I were riding bikes around our neighborhood when we spotted a group of guys from school. We tried to show off how awesome we were at ten-speed stunts, so Rachel popped a wheelie, then jumped her bike up and off a curb. I tried to do the same thing, but when I got to the curb, I didn't pull my bike up high enough and my front tire rammed into the curb, dumping me and my bike into the street. I guess the wind got knocked out of me because the next thing I remember was opening my eyes to everyone standing over me making sure I was still alive!

Frannie, 14, Ohio

It had just finished raining when my cousin and I went out to skate. We passed my crush's house, and he was outside with his three friends. While I was trying to impress him with my moves, I slipped in a puddle, rolled into a ditch, and landed in what I thought was mud. To my surprise, it was a pile of dog poop. Talk about humiliation!

Melissa, 14, Texas

I was expecting a call from this guy I'd had a crush on for months. When the phone rang, I answered, but it was my friend. As I was telling her how much I wanted him to call, I heard the beep for call waiting. I clicked over, and it was my crush! I told him I'd be right back, then as soon as I pressed the button to get back to my friend, I blurted out, "I am so excited. I really want to talk to him, but I desperately need to change my pad."

There was total silence, and then I realized—I had pressed the wrong button! I was still on the line with my crush. On Monday one of his friends came up to me and said, "You know, tampons can last up to three hours longer than pads before needing to be changed."

Natalie, 15, Pennsylvania

While I was performing a dance at my seventh-grade talent show, I noticed my crush sitting in the front row with his class. One of the steps we had to do was walk toward the front of the stage. I was looking at him and smiling. I guess I didn't realize how far down the stage I went because the next thing I knew, I was flat on my face with my crush helping me up from the floor. Now people call me "Humpty Dumpty."

Lora, 13, New York

My friends and I went to our marching band's annual band camp. One night during our free time, we thought it would be fun to spy on this boy I really liked. We had our cameras and everything! I was

MOST HUMILIATING
CRUSH CRASH

My freshman year, our whole high school went on an ice-skating trip. I had a major crush on this junior who I'd barely ever talked to. I was standing by the side of the rink, and I couldn't believe it when I noticed he was coming toward me. He skated up and said, "Hey, beautiful," holding out his hand. I was thrilled speechless and grabbed it, even though he was holding some keys. We skated around the rink a couple of times before he finally stopped and awkwardly told me that he was trying to get me to hold the keys for him so that he could skate with the really pretty girl who was standing next to me!

JENNIFER, 14, NEW YORK

peeking in the window to his dorm room and saw a guy I thought was him take off his pants, so I announced it to my friends. Suddenly they all started laughing, and I turned around to see none other than my guy standing there behind me with a smirk on his face. He said nothing and walked away, laughing. I could never look him in the eye again!

Diana, 15, Colorado

EDITOR'S NOTE: PRIVATE INVESTIGATOR WORK SHOULD NOT BE A CAREER CHOICE FOR DIANA!

I went to dinner with my boyfriend and his family (it was my first time meeting them). I was eating chicken wings when his brother told a joke. I started laughing so hard, I choked on the bone. I coughed it out, and it flew across the table, hitting his mom on the forehead. Needless to say, they haven't invited me back for dinner.

Trina, 19, Nevada

*I*t was Valentine's Day, and I wanted to give my crush

something special. I got him some heart-shaped chocolates that said, "I love you, will you go out with me?" I was in a hurry to give it to him and slipped the box into his locker. The next day a boy I didn't know said, "Yes!" with a big grin on his face. "Yes, what?" I asked. He held up the chocolates—I had put the box in the wrong locker!

Anna, 12, Oregon

I was at the prom and was telling my best friend about my crush. Suddenly the DJ announced that there was a dedication from my crush to . . . and he said my name! I started screaming and jumping up and down. The dance floor cleared, and I walked over to my crush. But when I got there, he said, "Why did you come out here? I wasn't talking about you. I meant the other Sara." I ran off the dance floor. That was the worst night ever.

Sara, 16, California

It was the beginning of our volleyball game, and my team was warming up. The whole school was there to watch, including the guy I liked. I decided to impress him with my athletic moves, so I kicked my foot up really high and didn't realize I was too close to the net. My foot got tangled in it, and I lost my balance and fell on my butt. Everyone, including my crush, laughed hysterically.

Jodi, 14, Nebraska

My crush and I have English class together, and he needed to borrow my notes. After I gave them to him, I realized that I'd written lovey-dovey stuff on my notebook about how much I like him and what a babe he is. He came by later to return my notes. I turned around quickly to run away 'cause I was too embarrassed to face him, and I smacked my head into my locker. So I ended up embarrassing myself to avoid facing humiliation!

Carrie, 15, New York

One day my dad and I went to the drugstore, and I spotted a total hottie working as a cashier. I was so busy checking him out and trying to make eye contact that I didn't notice the steps in front of me. I tripped on them and knocked down a huge Coke display. The guy came over to help me and to see if I was okay. I couldn't even talk, I was so mortified.

Kara, 14, Michigan

My crush and I were making pancakes in our home ec class. I tried to show off by flipping them high in the air, then catching them in the pan. I went to grab one, but my hand slipped, and instead I smacked him with the frying pan, knocking him straight to the floor. He got a big welt on his forehead and hasn't talked to me since.

Ally, 16, Connecticut

My mom and I went shopping for a new video camera. I was testing one of the display cameras and zooming in on objects in the store. I saw a group of cute guys from my school, so I focused on them. I even checked out their butts! After a while they started giving me weird looks, but I didn't know why. It turns out there was a big-screen TV right above me that showed the whole store what I was looking at with the camera.

Andrea, 15, California

EDITOR'S NOTE: AND THE ACADEMY AWARD FOR BEST BUTT SHOT GOES TO . . . ANDREA!

I wrote a love letter to a cute guy in my class, but I was too shy to give it to him. My friend told me he'd deliver the note for me. But as he was passing it to my crush, our teacher caught him. She read the entire note out loud to our class. Then she came over to my desk and said, "I believe this is yours," and tossed the note to me. How humiliating!

Janie, 12, Indiana

I had some friends leave a rose with a note around the stem saying, "Call me," with my phone number on my crush's doorstep. Later I got a phone call from his single mom! I hadn't written who the rose was to or from, and his mom thought the rose was from her crush! I told her she had the wrong number.

April, 18, California

Every year during Labor Day weekend our town hosts this huge fair. My crush invited me to go with him. It was our first "date" without any of our friends around. We took a couple of paddleboats out for a cruise around the fairgrounds. When we went under this bridge, he leaned over to kiss me. I playfully pulled away, causing the boat to tip over! Both of us fell into the water in front of a bunch of other boaters who were totally cracking up at us, plus there were a ton of people on the shore who were pointing and laughing. It was awful!

Stephanie, 13, Oklahoma

For my birthday my friends took me to this teen dance club. I am not a good dancer, and I was content to just hang out against the wall and watch everyone. But then this totally hot guy came over to me and said, "You are so beautiful. I have to dance with you."

MORTIFYING MOVIE MOMENTS

Big-screen humiliation is pretty common, which just goes to show how much we love to laugh when we're not the ones in the hot seat! Check out some of the all-time most embarrassing experiences that characters in these classic flicks faced.

SIXTEEN CANDLES: After bonding with her school's king of nerds, Ted, Samantha (played by Molly Ringwald) agrees to give him a pair of her panties. Then at the school dance Ted sets up a viewing station in the guys' bathroom, charging a dollar a head for a glimpse. Later that night Ted shows up at a party thrown by Samantha's crush, Jake. Ted proceeds to confess the whole story to Jake—and even hands over the prized panties! Samantha is beyond humiliated, but luckily the incident doesn't stop her from getting together with Jake.

CLUELESS: Cher (Alicia Silverstone) is trying her best to flirt with Christian on their video date, but he's completely oblivious. The harder she tries to impress him, the less he seems to notice. But he certainly can't miss it when her last-ditch effort to look cool goes wrong and she ends up falling over onto the floor! Cher and Christian don't end up together, but soon enough she realizes that he isn't the right guy for her, anyway.

GREASE: When Sandy (Olivia Newton-John) says good-bye to her summer love, Danny (John Travolta), she doesn't expect to see him again. That's why she's thrilled when she ends up transferring to his school that fall. Expecting him to be equally happy, she rushes over to talk to him. But to her serious embarrassment, Danny brushes her off big-time—trying to look cool in front of his friends. We all know that Danny's the one who should feel bad, not Sandy. How rude! But that doesn't stop Sandy from being pretty morti-fied. At least she makes Danny work hard to get her back!

He grabbed my hand to lead me to the dance floor, but I didn't want him to see I had two left feet. So I pulled away and ran off without even saying a word to him!

Kristen, 14, Kansas

EDITOR'S NOTE: ENROLL IN A DANCE CLASS—FAST! YOU DON'T WANT ANOTHER SWEET GUY TO GET AWAY.

My best friend scored the e-mail address of my crush. I typed up a possible note to send to him, then sent it off to my bud to get her vote of approval, along with a little note asking her if she thought it was too obvious that I was totally into him. Fifteen minutes later I got an e-mail from my crush, asking, "Uh . . . was this for me?" with the e-mail to my friend. I'd accidentally sent the e-mail to *him* instead!

Laynie, 14, Oregon

EDITOR'S NOTE: THE TRIBULATIONS OF MODERN TECHNOLOGY!

I went to a party at a friend's house and met her cute cousins who were visiting for the weekend. One of them asked me, "So, what class are you in?" I was totally baffled and said, "I'm not in a class!" They started cracking up. I was still confused until my friend came over and said, "What *grade* are you in?" I felt so dumb.

Randi, 15, Missouri

My first kiss was a major disaster. I was at camp, and the guy I'd had a crush on all summer invited me to go on a walk with him. We came to this really pretty waterfall and sat down right near it. It was beautiful. Then he leaned over to kiss me. His lips on mine felt so soft and smooth—it was great! Then I felt his tongue. I pulled away, wiped my mouth, and said, "What are you doing?!" Later his friends made fun of me for not knowing how to French kiss and said I should start practicing with pillows! I felt like such a little kid.

Meadow, 14, Missouri

HIS MOST
EMBARRASSING MOMENTS

Okay, here's proof that the gym class cutie has had his
share of mortification!

 I was on a first date with this cute girl from homeroom. On the way to the movies we were having a
great time, talking and joking, when my car suddenly
died. She helped me push it to the side of the road,
and I called a tow service. When the tow guy showed
up, he checked out the car, then said, "You should
check the fuel meter more regularly." I had forgotten
to fill the car up with gas!

David, 17, Arizona

My dad and I were having lunch at a nice
restaurant. Our waitress was this really pretty girl I
recognized from school. I thought I'd make a good

impression so that later I could ask her out. I was nice and flirty, but not obnoxious. I guess my dad could tell I was into her, so when we got the check, he said, "My son would like to ask you out, but he's too shy. So, will you go out with him?" I was so stunned that all I could do was stutter something like, "Uh-uh-duh-uh-huh," and nod. The girl laughed in my face! I ran out of the restaurant as fast as I could.

Justin, 15, Oregon

I sometimes baby-sit for this family friend of my mom's who has three little girls. One Saturday while I was sitting, the girls wanted to play dress up—actually they wanted to dress *me* up. It was a hot day, so we were out on the front porch, which was pretty well hidden from the street by bushes. I sat patiently while they applied makeup and played with my hair. When they were done, they wanted me to "model walk," so I got up and strutted across the porch, doing my best Kate Moss. Then I heard hysterical laughter. I looked down, and these girls from school were walking by—pointing and giggling at me. I smiled at them, then ducked and crawled back into the house. I was petrified! The girls now call me "Sheila."

Sheldon, 16, California

I was riding my bike to school when I saw this really hot girl. I was smiling at her, and she was grinning back at me. Suddenly I heard a car honking and screeching brakes. I had been so busy looking at her that I hadn't realized that I was riding into oncoming traffic! Talk about a first impression!

William, 14, Missouri

I was in line for some nachos at the mall food court. Waiting in front of me was one of the most beautiful girls I'd ever seen. She turned around and looked right at me, staring, so I smiled back. Then my friend came running up to me. He took one look at me and said,

"Dude, you've got a huge booger hanging out of your nose!" That's why she'd been staring at me!

Chris, 13, Illinois

My friend was having a pool party when my crush and a bunch of her hot friends showed up. I thought I'd be really cool and show off my diving. I did a perfect swan and hit the water like a knife. Then I came up and climbed out of the water. Everyone started busting up, and I didn't know why, so I looked down at myself. I had hit the water so hard, my bathing suit had come off and was still floating in the pool!

Dan, 15, Florida

Chapter Two:
Bud Bloopers

Making a fool of yourself with your friends can be fun once you've bonded. But when you're first getting to know each other, even one accidental burp can be pretty mortifying.

Plus sometimes your friends are the ones embarrassing *you*—which isn't always so funny. The best is when you and your friends can share the humiliation, like what happened to fourteen-year-old Jenni when she and her friends caused quite a scene at their local mall.

Check out these moments of spectacular silliness, and see if you and your buds can top 'em!

THE MORT-O-METER

Barely Blushing

Blushing Babe

Blush-O-Rama

I recently made friends with this new girl at school, who happens to have only one arm. We get along great and have a lot in common, and she's easy to joke with. I've gotten so comfortable around her that I don't even notice her handicap. One day I was complaining about how much I hated calculus, and she said she loved it. I responded by saying, "Yuck! I'd rather cut off my left arm than take calculus!" It came out so fast, I didn't have time to stop it. Luckily she burst out laughing, but I was mortified.

Amber, 17, Kentucky

I was at a party with a bunch of my friends. My crush was there, and we went outside on the porch and started making out. Suddenly we heard all this laughter coming from inside. When we looked up, we noticed that the porch light was creating this projected image of us kissing on the wall inside the house. Everyone had seen us making out! My friends never let me live that down.

Kelly, 16, California

EDITOR'S NOTE: TALK ABOUT A LOVE SCENE!

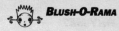

My best friend and I were at this gourmet food shop with my mom, and we were checking out the counter. I thought I saw some sample cups of drinks on a table because the last time I was at this store, they'd had samples out. I went over, picked one up, and started to drink it. But it was a candle—luckily it wasn't lit! The people at the counter stared at me, like, "What are you doing?" I was so embarrassed, I ran out of the store!

KC, 11, North Carolina

Some friends and I were hanging out at the movie theater one night and started talking to a couple of guys. We had to go because our ride had just pulled up, so I said good-bye and started to run to the car. I turned my head to yell at my friends to hurry up and ran right into a pole! I fell to the ground, and when I looked up, I saw a bunch of people from my school staring at me, including the hot guys I met and all their friends!

Nima, 15, Montana

Four of us were hanging out at my friend Bethany's house. Bethany's parents weren't home, so we were playing the stereo superloud. An 'N Sync song came on, so we lined up and started pretending we were the guys in concert, getting totally into it. When the song was over, we heard hysterical laughter coming from outside. We ran out front to find Bethany's older brother, her boyfriend, and my crush rolling around on the lawn, totally cracking up. Turns out they were spying on us through the window and had caught our whole act!

Kayla, 14, California

I was eating at the mall with my girlfriends, but one girl was last coming over with her tray. While she was walking in our direction, she tripped over an empty baby stroller, and her chili fries went flying everywhere. My friends and I were laughing so hard that one friend spit her drink out, another broke her ring on the table, and another actually wet her pants! Everyone in the entire food court was staring at us.

Jenni, 14, Massachusetts

What Do You Do if Your Friend Does Something That Totally Embarrasses You?

According to California-based parenting instructor Cookie Spancer, first you have to evaluate the situation and figure out if the embarrassing moment was truly humiliating. "Sometimes we're just a little too sensitive," says Cookie. "You might be the kind of person who embarrasses much more easily than other people."

If you aren't being overly sensitive and really were embarrassed badly by your bud, Cookie offers this advice: "You should be totally honest and confront her. Make sure you say something like, 'I care about you and our friendship, but what you said or did really embarrassed me.' It's important that she knows you are upset but that you don't want to give up on the friendship."

Cookie also points out that there are some people who will embarrass you over and over again and won't ever get a clue that what they're doing is hurtful. "These people don't know any better," says Cookie. "For some reason, they just are the way they are—it could be that everyone in their family is also that way and that's just how they learned to relate to people." In those situations Cookie suggests definitely confronting your friend but warns that she might not recognize her insensitivity or change. "In some instances you may want to reconsider the friendship," advises Cookie.

My best friend and I were at the mall. I saw this really cute guy standing near the yogurt shop. When we passed by him, my bud pushed me into him and said, "She thinks you're cute." He was eating yogurt, and when I bumped him, it spilled all over both of us. I can't believe my friend did that to me! I was so embarrassed.

Natalie, 12, Wyoming

I was staying over at my best friend's house, and I woke up in the middle of the night, starving. I tried to wake up my friend, but she was fast asleep. I tip-toed very quietly out into the kitchen and started rummaging through the cupboards. I didn't turn on the lights because I didn't want to wake anyone up. In the dark I pulled out a bag of potato chips from the pantry. Suddenly the lights flipped on, and my friend's dad called out, "Who's in here with the lights off?" I was so scared that the chip bag flew out of my hands, spilling chips all over the kitchen and all over my friend's dad, who had come downstairs for a mid-

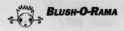
night snack. Now my friend's family calls me "Raccoon" because I was scrounging around for food.

Midge, 13, New York

had just gotten my driver's license, and I was taking my friends out for a spin. We decided to cruise through the mall parking lot. Going out the driveway, I drove over those teethlike spikes that keep people from going in through the out driveway. One of my friends yelled, "Wait! What did that sign say?" I panicked and backed up, popping all of the tires on my mom's car. The sign said, DO NOT BACK UP. SEVERE TIRE DAMAGE. My friends could not stop laughing at me.

Hanna, 16, New Mexico

had just gotten a Bee Gees CD, and I was listening to the track "Stayin' Alive" over and over again in my headphones—thinking I was in my own private world and no one would ever know how many times in a row I listened to the tune. (I just couldn't get enough of that song!) Suddenly I felt someone lift the phones off my ears and sing one of the lines. I turned around. My best friend and her sister were cracking up. "How many times are you gonna listen to that song?!" they asked. I guess I had been singing along really loudly, and they'd been in my doorway watching me for at least three repeats.

Summer, 15, Maine

One partyless Friday night my friends and I decided to have a girls-only night. We walked up to this restaurant in our neighborhood that turned out to be a little too pricey for us, but we didn't know that until we were sitting down, checking out the menus. We only had about $10 each! Our waiter was this older, way cute Brendan Fraser look-alike. He went over the specials and took a lot of time looking each one of us in the eye while he explained the details of the salmon with fennel cream sauce. When he asked for our orders, I stupidly blurted out, "We can't afford anything but the soup!" He gave me a really weird look, and I felt so stupid. My friends were trying to duck under the table. Luckily he treated us just like the rest of the customers and even gave us free samples of some appetizers!

Lauren, 14, Oregon

WHAT DO YOU DO IF YOU DO SOMETHING THAT TOTALLY EMBARRASSES YOUR FRIEND?

Cookie Spancer says that the first thing you should do is be honest and apologize as soon as you recognize your mistake. If you're hanging out and you let something slip that you know embarrassed your friend, make it up to her right then and there. "That way you'll take the attention off of her and put it all on you," advises Cookie.

If you don't realize until later that you probably went overboard, call your friend immediately and let her know how sorry you are and that you won't let it happen again. If you're a little shy or afraid to 'fess up and face your pal because you think she's going to be mad, Cookie recommends bringing along another friend. "That way you'll have someone with you to offer courage and support and be a witness to the fact that you have honestly tried to make amends," she says.

Last year both my best friend and I didn't have dates on Valentine's Day, so we decided to spend the day together. I'm a pretty good cook, and I decided to bake a chicken using one of Martha Stewart's recipes that I'd never tried before. I thought for sure I followed it exactly, but after two hours of the chicken not getting any browner and several rechecks of the recipe, I realized that I had never turned the oven on! I was totally embarrassed—especially after making such a big deal about what a great cook I was!

Cali, 17, Louisiana

My parents were out of town for a week, and a friend of theirs was staying at our house to watch me and my little brother. On Friday night I begged her to go out so that I could have some friends over. She agreed and went to a movie. I had about five girls over and we rented some movies. But I had forgotten to get the proper snacks. My friend Kelli offered to drive up to the store, but I said, "That's okay; I'll drive." I only had my permit, but I thought it would be a good time to practice—and of course *nothing would happen*. All was well until I hit the 7-Eleven parking lot. I

MOST HUMILIATING BUD BLUNDER

I was at a school dance with a bunch of my friends. A few of us were in the bathroom together, and one of my buds was trying to make me spill the beans on my crush. I didn't want to budge, but she said if I didn't confess, they would tell everyone I liked this other guy, who I wasn't interested in at all. Finally I told her, and she rushed out of the bathroom straight to the DJ. She grabbed the mike away from him and said, "This next song goes out to Jodi and Jeff," revealing my crush to everyone!

JODI, 15, WISCONSIN

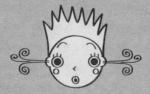

EDITOR'S NOTE: MEAN FRIEND ALERT! JODI, FIND OUT WHAT HER DEAL IS BECAUSE SHE'S ACTING TOTALLY UN-FRIEND WORTHY!

pulled into a spot, but instead of hitting the brakes, I pressed harder on the accelerator and the car went screaming through the store window, breaking the glass. Luckily Kelli pulled the emergency brake and we stopped just inside without hitting anyone. My parents' friend gave me a huge lecture about trust and responsibility, and then I got in serious trouble when my parents got home from vacation.

Tammy, 15, Oregon

Our school has this annual ski trip. Somehow I got on a chair lift with the most popular girl in school. She turned out to be really cool and nice, and we were starting to hit it off by the time it was our turn to get off the lift. As I started to move forward, getting ready to jump, I noticed that my ski pants were caught on the chair somehow. I didn't want to look stupid by asking for help, so I just stayed on the lift, pretending like I'd only meant to come along for the ride. I rode the lift up and down at least three more times before I was finally able to untangle myself. The popular girl looked at me like I was crazy the whole rest of the trip.

Melinda, 15, Utah

Every year my family stays at a house on the beach. Last summer I brought my best friend along. We met these really hot guys on the beach one day and agreed to hang out with them on the boardwalk later that night. All day my friend and I talked about how cute the guys were and decided which one we should go for. But when we met up with the guys, they looked so different out of bathing suits that I couldn't remember who my guy was and ended up flirting with my bud's guy! I felt like a total jerk.

Janice, 15, California

It was a Sunday morning. My friend and I were lounging around at her house, having breakfast and reading the comics. She has a dog that I'm a little bit allergic to, so I kept scratching my face. All of a sudden her dad came in to get some of the newspaper, took one look at me, and burst out laughing. Then my friend looked up and started cracking up. "Hey, Inky," her dad said. I ran to the bathroom to look in the mirror. I had gotten newsprint all over my face from reading the comics and then scratching! They've never let me live that down.

Lacey, 16, Massachusetts

One of our friends was really sick, so another friend and I decided to cheer her up by baking her some cookies and putting them in a really pretty tin. Neither one of us is a very good cook, and this time was no exception. All of the cookies burned. We decided to give them to her, anyway, figuring she would be too sick to eat them but would still appreciate the thought. When we went to see her, she must have been feeling much better because she immediately grabbed the tin from me and said, "Ooh, cookies," opened it, and started eating before we could say a word. Her face wrinkled in disgust, and she spit out the burned cookie pieces.

Shana, 14, Alabama

My friend and I were supposed to meet in front of the West Lane Theaters at four o'clock to see a movie. When my dad dropped me off, she wasn't there yet, so I waited for her. And waited. And waited. After an

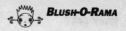
hour I called her house and left a really angry message on her answering machine, then called my dad to come pick me up. When I got home, my friend called me and asked where I'd been. She'd been waiting for me at the West *Gate* Theaters for two hours! Talk about a misunderstanding!

Jennifer, 12, Oregon

We were at the mall when my bud spotted an old friend of hers and introduced me. "This is Rachel," I thought she said. We hung out with her for the rest of the afternoon—shopping, scoping babes, having lunch. Rachel was really cool, and I kept saying stuff like, "We should hang out with Rachel more often," and "Oh, Rachel, you'd look cute in that," or "Rachel, that guy looks like your type." When we finally parted, my friend turned to me and said, "I didn't want to embarrass you, but her name is April, not Rachel." I couldn't believe it! I felt like a total dork.

Monique, 15, New Hampshire

EDITOR'S NOTE: MONIQUE, IT'S APRIL'S FAULT— SHE SHOULD HAVE CORRECTED YOU RIGHT AWAY. OR YOUR BUD COULD HAVE PULLED YOU ASIDE AND LET YOU KNOW.

I was showing off a new move I'd just learned in dance class in front of my friends. We had the music blasting, and I was getting totally into it. About halfway through the routine, there's a spin. When I spun around, I was going too fast and ran smack into the wall, which knocked me flat on the floor. My friends were cracking up. That's the last time I practice my dance routine in front of them!

Buffi, 15, Idaho

We were at a really crowded concert when one of my friends became separated from the rest of us. I called out to her, but she didn't hear me. I ran through the crowd and grabbed at her and pulled. Then I heard this horrible ripping sound. I had grabbed her really expensive black pants (the ones she'd saved up for for months!) and ripped them. I felt so bad.

Gwendolyn, 16, New York

SEVEN WAYS TO MAKE IT UP TO A FRIEND THAT YOU'VE TOTALLY MORTIFIED

1. Tell everyone who witnessed the moment that it was your fault, not hers.

2. Bake her a batch of delicious cookies and attach a note letting her know what a great pal she is and how much you love her.

3. Take her to a movie or invite her over to watch her favorite video.

4. Record that CD of yours that she's been dying to get.

5. Bring her a bright bouquet of forget-me-nots.

6. Dedicate a song to her on the radio.

7. Say you're sorry over and over.

Chapter Three:
School Snafus

Of all the places to make a total clod out of your-self—besides maybe the mall—school has got to be the worst. You spend most of your time there, and it's definitely where you make your biggest and most lasting impressions. It's also where a reputation can fade or be made.

But embarrassment can strike anywhere, any-time—during sports, in class, at lunch, or by your locker. You could even be taking a harmless stroll down the hallway like Heather, 15, from New Jersey, was doing when her humiliation struck. Read on to see what happened to her and everyone else's school snafus!

THE MORT-O-METER

A NEW 'DO WILL MAKE 'EM FORGET IT WAS YOU.

KEEP A LOW PROFILE FOR THE NEXT COUPLE OF DAYS.

JOIN THE WITNESS PROTECTION PROGRAM.

My very first day of seventh grade in first-period history class, I made myself look like a complete idiot. My teacher asked the class if anyone had any relatives outside the country. I raised my hand, along with a few other people, and she asked us to stand up. Other kids named off countries as I waited for my turn. When the teacher finally called on me, I piped up, "New Mexico," and sat down. Everyone was looking at me strangely. The teacher said, "Uh, New Mexico is a state, dear." I was totally mortified—for some reason when she said "country," I thought she meant "state." What a great way to start seventh grade!

Jenna, 14, California

Right around the same time I was working on this term paper for my English class, I also got together with a guy I'd liked for a long time. I wrote this really mushy note to him the night before I turned in my paper—and somehow I accidentally turned in the note with the paper! When I got it back from my English teacher, there was this big question mark at the top. I wanted to die.

Judy, 16, New York

I was in the locker room changing into my gym clothes when my best friend grabbed me and pushed me out into the hallway. (We pull pranks on each other all the time and are always trying to outdo each other. She was getting back at me for shoving her into the pool the day before while she was fully dressed.) Just as I hit the hallway, the principal happened to be walking by, and he saw me in my bra and underwear! He pretended not to notice and kept on going. I was sooo embarrassed!

Tina, 15, New York

EDITOR'S NOTE: HOPEFULLY TINA WAS WEARING HER GOOD UNDIES!

My best bud and I always sit at the same table in the cafeteria. This one day I got my lunch and sat in our usual spot. My friend was already sitting down.

I wasn't really paying attention to her because there was this very cute guy sitting at the table next to ours and I was checking him out. With my eyes still on him, I reached over and grabbed some fries off my friend's tray. Then this unfamiliar voice said, "Hey! Those are mine!" I looked over at my "friend" and realized it wasn't her—it was someone I didn't know!

Janet, 14, Florida

Our school put on this production of *The Pirates of Penzance*, and I got to be the lead. I was really psyched because I tried hard for the part. On opening night I was way confident—I knew I was going to be a huge hit. In the first act I had to draw my sword for this fight scene, which I had practiced to death. But this time when I went to draw my sword, it was stuck. I kept tugging, trying to maintain my cool, but it wouldn't budge. I had to play the scene with an air sword, which looked ridiculous. All of my fellow actors and the audience laughed so hard at me!

Shana, 16, Illinois

I go to a private school where we have to wear uniforms. At lunch one day someone bumped me, and I spilled juice all over the white front of my uniform. I went into the administration office to see if I could get cleaned off somehow, and the principal made me put on the school's only spare uniform, which happened to be the kind for guys. We had a sub in history that afternoon, and the teacher kept thinking I was a boy! The whole class called me "sir" for months afterward!

Lily, 14, Michigan

I had to give this presentation to the whole school assembly. I practiced over and over again in front of the wall at home, lifting my head to make eye contact with my audience, smiling at the right moments, and putting emphasis on just the right syllables. When it was my turn to present at the assembly, I automatically turned to face the wall instead of the audience and ended up starting to give the speech to the wall, eye contact and all, just like I'd practiced. Luckily I caught myself and turned to the real audience, but my face was red from blushing the whole time, and I could see people snickering at me. Talk about humiliating!

Becky, 16, North Carolina

One day during gym I made a trip to the bathroom, then came back out and got in line with everyone else. The whole class, one at a time, had to climb the ropes. During my turn, with the entire class watching, everyone started laughing because I had a long piece of toilet paper hanging out of my shorts! I was so mortified, plus the story made its way around the whole school.

Deanne, 12, Rhode Island

Last year at prom my date got up on the table and started dancing. He said, "I would like to dedicate this dance to my date," and he did the funky chicken! Now everyone calls me "Funky Chicken."

Bette, 17, Illinois

SORRIEST
SCHOOL SNAFU

Our marching band had a big show during the homecoming game halftime. I was on color guard and I was really nervous since it was my first performance. As I was spinning the flag around, it flew out of my grip and hit the color guard captain on the head, knocking her to the ground. The whole show had to stop, and she had to be carried off the field. I was so mortified, I tried to quit the team the next day!

RACHEL, 15, ARIZONA

I was walking across the cafeteria when I slipped on something wet. Looking for something to hold on to as I was falling, I grabbed the backpack of this cute guy in front of me. But we both ended up falling to the ground. He wasn't too happy with me, and even worse, the stuff I slipped in was someone's vomit!

Naomi, 16, Oregon

EDITOR'S NOTE: JUST THINK HOW EMBARRASSED THE PERSON WHO ACTUALLY THREW UP MUST HAVE BEEN. YUCK!

My boyfriend and I were at a school dance, and we went to the vending machine to get some sodas. I didn't notice that someone had spilled punch on the chair next to the vending machine, so I sat down, and the punch ended up soaking into my white dress. I walked around at the dance for a while before I realized that people were pointing and laughing at me. When I finally saw the huge stain, I ran home, crying. The next day at school people threw tampons at me.

Jilian, 15, Illinois

*O*ne night I stupidly decided to dedicate a love song to my crush on the radio. I called in, made it onto the radio, and confessed my true feelings. I told the DJ my name and how much I adored my crush. The next day in history class we were supposed to bring in some kind of current news event—it could be a newspaper or magazine clipping, something taped off TV, anything as long as it was news. Well, the guy who sits behind me brought a cassette tape to class. He popped it in the tape player, and I heard a familiar voice—mine! He'd been listening to the radio station the night before and had recorded my confession, the love song, everything! Now when people from my class see me, they start singing the song.

Katie, 15, Michigan

*M*y cheerleading squad was performing at a pep rally at school. I rushed out of the locker room to take my spot on the floor. As I hurried out, I could hear people laughing and yelling my name. I saw my boyfriend signaling something to me, but I couldn't tell what he was saying. We performed our dance routine, then ran off the court and back to the locker room. Then I finally realized what everyone was laughing about. My skirt was tucked into my underwear!

Sable, 14, Louisiana

'm on the swim team, and one of the things the coach has us do is drink a *lot* of milk. One Friday after practice, I downed half a carton and then stuck the carton in my locker to save the rest for later. When we came to school on Monday, the whole place smelled like a trillion stink bombs had gone off. It was so bad that I complained to the principal in front of everyone and said no one could go to class until it was cleared up. All of the students were sent outside to wait while the principal and the janitor searched the school. The culprit was a half-full carton of Knudsen milk—found in my locker! I was beyond mortified and vowed silence for at least three weeks. The whole school still calls me "Knudsen."

Sue, 16, Illinois

I was headed home from school with my friend, and I wanted to show her the new move that I had just learned at cheerleading practice. I started the cheer, and toward the end I had to do a big kick. As I kicked, my shoe flew off my foot and hit the guy who was walking in front of us. When he turned around, I saw that he was the hottest guy in school!

Kayla, 13, Ohio

EDITOR'S NOTE: KAYLA, HOW ABOUT TRYING OUT FOR THE SOCCER TEAM?

My best friend had a pretty bad breakup with her boyfriend. As I was leaving my home ec class one afternoon, I spotted him heading toward me down the hall. I was pretty mad at him for the way he'd treated my friend, so I started giving him the evil eye, burrowing into him with my laser gaze. The next thing I knew, I was sliding down the hall and smacked right into him! I had slipped on this napkin

FIVE WAYS TO NOT CARE WHAT ANYONE THINKS ABOUT YOU

It's pretty tough to be completely immune to other people's opinions of you, especially when they don't bother hiding their thoughts! But here are some things to keep in mind when you find yourself obsessing a little too much over the impressions an embarrassing incident might have left on someone:

1. YOU CAN'T PLEASE EVERYONE ALL THE TIME.

You are never going to make every single person thrilled with all the stuff you do and say every moment of the day, so stop trying. That doesn't mean you should start acting like a jerk, but just realize that it's not your responsibility to make everybody else happy.

2. YOU DON'T HAVE TO BE FRIENDS WITH EVERYONE.

So that girl whose gym locker is next to yours saw you do something silly and hasn't talked to you since? Don't worry about her! Having friends is great, but you're going to meet people sometimes that you just don't click with, and that's okay. There's no rule that you have to get along with every single person in the universe. If someone holds your one bad moment against you forever, then she doesn't have good friend potential, anyway.

3. ■ ***STAY TRUE TO YOURSELF.*** Being yourself all the time can be extremely difficult, especially when people around you make you feel that you should act a certain way. But if you stick to who you are and keep doing what you like to do, then in the end the most important person will be happy—you.

4. ■ ***BE CONFIDENT.*** Easier said than done, definitely. But if you feel good about yourself, other people will feel good about you, too. How can they stay focused on one thing you did when you're obviously way past it? And even if someone does keep bugging you, you won't care because *you'll* know you're worth a lot more.

5. ■ ***KEEP BUSY.*** When will you have time to worry about what everyone's thinking if you're running from one activity to another? Don't overload yourself to the point of major stress, but give yourself enough fun things to do that you can't obsess over things that you can't change.

that had butter on it. What an impression—he just laughed at me!

Heather, 15, New Jersey

e were watching an old movie in my English class—*Breakfast at Tiffany's*, with Audrey Hepburn, which is one of my faves. I know a lot of the lines by heart, so I was mouthing along with the flick when my teacher turned the sound down on the movie and said, "Amanda, do you have something important to say?" Everyone turned to look at me. I wanted to slide under my desk!

Amanda, 13, Wisconsin

'm one of three announcers on our daily student bulletin—it's a school news report that gets broadcast to the whole school between first and second periods. Most of the time we're pretty calm and collected, but for some reason this one day we could not stop laughing. We were barely able to get through the class and club news without totally cracking up. At the end of each report we take turns signing off, wishing our fellow classmates a "fab Friday" or "manic Monday" or whatever. This particular day was my turn to sign off. Usually I try to think of an adjective way before we even start broadcasting, but I had totally forgotten this time. I was halfway into, "This is Amy, wishing you a . . . ," when I realized I had no idea what I was going to say and quickly blurted out the first nonword I could think of, "Uh, uh, THRIPINDICULAR THURSDAY!" My fellow announcers totally lost it, falling off their stools, and screaming with laughter into the mikes.

Amy, 17, California

had to write a poem for English class, and I wrote about this time I saw a couple fighting in a parking lot, from the girl's point of view. I really didn't think anything about it until my teacher read it aloud in class and praised me for being so deep and thoughtful. Then she said something totally hokey: "It was like a well, full of musty water, old shoes, a lost ring— forgotten dreams and promises . . . ," going on and on. A few kids in the class started laughing, and now they call me "The Well." I hope my teacher never reads one of my poems aloud again!

Dawn, 16, Texas

At my school freshmen are treated like dogs—lower than low. Our lockers are set up so that there are four in each column. Freshmen start with the bottom locker, sophomores above that, and so on. So, I have a bottom locker that I practically have to lie on the floor to get into every day. One day I came into school to find the senior guy whose locker is all the way at the top above mine pointing at my locker and cracking up with his friends. When they saw me, they started laughing even harder. I bent down to my locker, and I noticed that someone had put a "Loser" sticker on the front! It turned out to be my brother, who's friends with those guys! To make it worse, he superglued it on there to be sure it wouldn't come off.

Heather, 14, Washington, D.C.

I'm not very good at sports, but swimming is the worst. One day in swim class I was doing the backstroke, thinking about this guy I like in homeroom, imagining us living happily ever after, when all of a sudden I heard shouting and then—BANG!—my head hit the wall, and I blacked out. When I came to, the swim coach was fanning me, holding me in the water, and all my classmates surrounded us. Then I found out that the coach had jumped in the water with all his clothes on to save me!

Carrie, 14, California

EDITOR'S NOTE: THIS IS DEFINITELY ONE OF THOSE SITUATIONS WHERE EYES IN THE BACK OF YOUR HEAD WOULD COME IN HANDY!

It was the first week of seventh-grade gym class. We had just come into the locker room after a long, sweaty game of volleyball. I was about to open my locker when I realized the combination was written down on a piece of paper that was now locked inside my locker! My gym teacher made everyone stop changing and called in the janitor to cut off the lock. Everyone was really annoyed that they couldn't get in the shower.

Sandra, 12, Hawaii

Every year my friends and I do a lip-synching act at our school talent show. This year was gonna be the best ever because we'd been practicing for months. I was the lead singer (we were pretending to be the seventies band Blondie). I had all my moves down. On the night of the show, as I moved across the stage, I was feeling pretty good, so I decided to add an extra little jump. But I ended up jumping right off the stage, landing on my ankle and breaking it!

Ashley, 16, Arizona

How to Rise Above a Rep

So, everyone calls you Blue because of the time you decided to get creative and dye your hair blond but it turned turquoise for one very long week.

Whatever you did to earn yourself that cute nickname or wacky reputation, realize that you can rise above it. According to northern California child development expert Claudia Simon, it won't last. "In most cases, people forget about the incident right away. There's always some new gossip to take its place. So whatever you did will be forgotten. Until then, hold your head up high and don't let it bother you," advises Claudia. "If you score a nickname that's kind of cool, use it to your advantage. Introduce yourself as the nickname and tell the story about how you got it. If you laugh it off, others will, too."

If you just can't seem to shake the rep with other people, you're going to have to try to at least let it go within yourself. It's only a real problem if *you're* still carrying around the image in your head. "You have to forgive yourself first and forget about other people. You don't need everyone to be your best friend."

Chapter Four:
Fam Foul-ups

No matter how hip Mom and Dad try to be, they are never cool enough to avoid embarrassing you at least once in a while. Throw Grandma and Grandpa, Fido, and a sib or two into the mix and the opportunities for humiliation skyrocket.

Some of you will probably be able to empathize with poor 16-year-old Sandi, who was majorly mortified in front of her best buds by her grandmother's goof.

Check out these truly timeless tales and see how your family rates—are you shacked up with the Simpsons or the Salingers?

THE MORT-O-METER

Minor Mortification

More Mortification

Major Mortification

My family was staying at this really fancy hotel. One morning my little sister and I were taking the elevator down to breakfast. The elevator was packed with people. For some reason my sis decided to be "funny" and let loose with her new favorite toy—a whoopee cushion she'd won at a nearby carnival. All the adults were clearly disgusted and backed away from us, and I just pretended I didn't know her. When the elevator doors opened, I tried to jam out of there and away from my sister, but my hair got caught on this man's coat button. I had to stand there untangling it while my sister continued to serenade us with her gross noises!

Lara, 16, Florida

I had just started going out with my new boyfriend and invited him to come home with me after school. I really wanted to impress him with how funky my room is and how cool my parents are. But when we got to my house, I opened the door to find my mom walking around in her bra and underwear!

Amber, 15, California

MOST FAB-O FAM FOUL-UP

While spending a day with my family and friends, I ate a lot of chocolate. The next day I was very constipated. When I told my mom, she went to the store to buy something for my "problem." While she was gone, my boyfriend, friends, and their boyfriends came over, and we were all hanging out on the porch. My mom came home, and five minutes later my little sister ran outside and said to me, "Mommy said if you're still constipated to come inside and take this stuff." I turned beet red.

MAGGIE, 13, OHIO

My mom and I were driving home from grocery shopping when my mom's favorite (lame) song came on. She turned it up, then started singing and bopping her head to it! At a stoplight we pulled up next to this car of really cute guys. When they looked over and saw my mom, they all started busting up. I sank as low as I could in my seat and hoped they didn't see me.

Kirsten, 16, California

A group of us were playing truth or dare at a sleepover. On my turn I was dared to moon the next car that passed. We went outside, and as soon as we saw the headlights, my pants came down. A few minutes later my parents got home, and my dad asked me if there was a "full moon out tonight." I was so embarrassed that I had mooned my parents!

Jina, 14, California

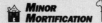 

My new boyfriend and I were getting ready to go for a walk in the park when my mom stopped us and asked if we could return some books for her. We said sure, and being the gentleman that he is, my bf took the books. As we neared the drop box at the library, we started looking through the books to see what Mom had checked out. They were books on sex, periods, and menopause! My boyfriend totally started cracking up—especially when he saw how red my face was!

Alison, 15, Oregon

I was walking my family's dog and decided to cruise past my crush's house. I was going to be very discreet. But when we got to his house, Dukie decided to do his duty on my crush's lawn! He was taking forever, and by the time he finally finished, my crush showed up with a couple of his friends! "Ew, why are you letting your dog go on our lawn?" he asked. Then I had to clean it up in front of them. I ran all the way home, humiliated. That's the last time I'm going to walk Dukie!

Bonnie, 13, Ohio

(71)

My mom and dad had a special birthday dinner for me and invited my grandparents. I invited three of my best buds who had never met my grandparents. When I introduced my grandma to my friend Syd, she turned to me, winking, and said, "Oh, he's so handsome!" She thought short-haired Syd was my boyfriend! I was horrified.

Sandi, 16, Tennessee

My mom and I were grocery shopping in the "feminine protection" section when a couple of the popular girls turned down the aisle. I was just about to say hi to them when my mom called out, "Stacy, do you need any maxi pads?" I think the whole store heard her! The popular girls burst out laughing and quickly passed me by.

Stacy, 14, Minnesota

EDITOR'S NOTE: "EMBARRASSED DAUGHTER ON AISLE 5 NEEDS IMMEDIATE ATTENTION!"

We were out to dinner at a fancy restaurant for my dad's birthday. The waiter was this cute guy who had graduated from my high school the year before. Just as he was starting to read off the specials, my six-year-old brother ripped a tremendous fart. It was the loudest one I'd ever heard and seemed to echo throughout the restaurant. There was a slight pause, then the waiter continued as if nothing had happened. A few seconds later my little bro said, "PEW!" and the stinkiest odor possible drifted through the air. This time the waiter stopped, wrinkled his nose, and said, "I'll be back in a minute." I wanted to slide under the table.

Glory, 16, Arkansas

I was on a date with this guy, and we were at my house watching TV, sitting close to each other on the couch. From out of nowhere my cat zooms across the room, under the couch, then reaches up a clawed paw and grabs my date right between his legs. My date screamed in pain and had to pry my cat's claws off of

DEALING WITH THE ADDAMS FAMILY

Everyone's family is a little wacky. Not one family is perfect, which is what makes us all unique and special and blah, blah—you already know that, right?

But still, how do you deal when your brother blurts out how "in love" you are with your crush—in front of him? Or when your sister tells your friends stories from when you were a baby or your mom calls out your AA bra size really loudly to the saleslady while a couple of the popular girls are walking by?

Okay, number one: Remember that your crush, those popular girls, and the entire public have parents, or brothers and sisters, or grandparents, or cousins, or aunts and uncles . . . and they've probably been embarrassed by one or all of them at some point.

Then take into consideration that most of the time your family really doesn't mean to embarrass you. It just happens. Think about it—you've probably embarrassed them plenty over the years. How about the time when you were one and right in the middle of your dad changing your diaper you pooped all over him in front of his buddies, who were there watching the game with him? Or the time your parents brought you along to dinner at their friends' house and you screamed your head off until they finally had to take you home? See? The list could go on and on.

The key is to lighten up a little and realize that no one, not even your family, is perfect—and that's okay.

However, if members of your family continuously embarrass you *intentionally* in a hurtful way, parenting instructor Cookie Spancer advises that you tell them right away that what they're doing is hurting you. "Let them know exactly what bothered you and why and make them understand that it really hurt you. Be serious and reasonable, and they should understand and be willing to make things better," she says.

him. "That's why I hate cats!" he yelled. We haven't been out since.

Neysa, 16, California

My first boyfriend and I were making out in the living room with the lights off. We were so into what we were doing (just kissing!) that we didn't hear my parents come in. All of a sudden the lights came on, and I heard laughing. "Looks like Abby's gonna win this one!" my dad yelled. "Ten points for sucking face!" my mom added. I was totally embarrassed. I wish they would have grounded me instead of standing there making fun of us.

Abbigail, 15, Milwaukee

My best friend was spending the night at my house, and we decided to sneak out to meet up with some other friends. We woke up at midnight and were just jumping out the window (my room is in the front of the house) when this car drove up in the driveway, blinding us with its headlights. My mom

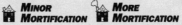

got out and said, "What are you doing?" She'd gone to the store to get some medicine for my dad's stomachache. I haven't tried to sneak out since!

Mandy, 14, Delaware

 I was talking to my best friend on the phone one afternoon, going on and on about my crush, Josh. I went into supersloppy details: what it might be like to kiss him, what our kids' names would be, what kind of wedding we would have. . . . At dinner that night my little brother told my parents that I was getting married in June and would be having three kids with Josh. I was furious! He had been listening in on the whole conversation.

Jodi, 13, Montana

My mom and dad took me and a couple of friends to a Limp Bizkit concert, but they sat far away from us. Our seats were next to these really cute college guys. Even though we were only fourteen, we told the guys we were all sixteen, thinking that after the show we'd never see them again and it wouldn't matter. After the concert we met up with my parents and were heading to the parking lot. That's when those college guys showed up. They asked us to follow them to this diner nearby for coffee. My dad piped up and offered to drop us off. One of the guys said, "Oh, but you're sixteen. I thought you could drive." My mom blurted out, "Sixteen? They're only fourteen." The guys looked at us like we were so lame and walked away.

Kelli, 14, Illinois

My older brother has a lot of very good-looking friends, and I have semicrushes on all of them. One day my brother brought a new friend over who's much nerdier than his other friends. Still a cool guy, but I'm not attracted to him in the least. To be funny, my bro told this guy I have the hots for him. Now every time he sees me, he's superflirty and nice. My brother laughs the whole time—he thinks it's a riot.

Stina, 15, New Mexico

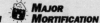

I was at this outdoor fair with my aunt when she spotted a couple of teenage boys hanging out at the snack bar. My aunt grabbed my wrist and said, "Oh, honey, those boys are total hunks! I bet one of them would love you!" Then she dragged me over to the snack bar. As we were ordering a couple of sodas, my aunt turned to one of them and winked. Pointing at me, she said, "You should really ask her out. She's worth it." I was totally embarrassed. To top it off, neither one of the guys was my type at all. Thank goodness they didn't take her seriously!

Ginny, 16, Nevada

I was in the backseat of my grandparents' car when I stretched my arms up over my head. It was a hot day, so I was wearing a tank top. My little brother was sitting next to me and poked me under the arm, squealing, "Ew, armpit hair!" Then my grandma started commenting on the fact that I was also getting "boobies." My grandpa chimed in with, "Won't be long

HOW TO SURVIVE THE FAMILY VACATION

The absolute best way to deal with family vacation drama is to stay home! Okay, since you probably can't do that, here are some coping skills from Cookie Spancer that should help you endure the potential embarrassment risks of going away with your family:

• Before you even leave, sit down with your family and let everyone know what kinds of things you do and don't want to do on the vacation—like no Civil War museums or lots of clothes shopping. Be willing to listen to what everyone else wants and realize that you will have to compromise. Maybe during a few of the outings that you're not so into, you can create an alternate plan for yourself. The more things you can figure out before you hit the road, the better your vacation will be.

• Realize that plans might have to change a bit here and there because of unforeseen problems like rain, a flat tire, or someone getting sick. Try to remain as flexible as possible.

• Talk about money and how and when it will be spent. Are

you bringing your savings for souvenirs? Are Mom and Dad giving you a vacation allowance? Knowing what you can spend will make it easier for you to create a budget.

• Don't argue with your parents about taking pics. They're gonna do it, anyway—even if you don't like your I-just-woke-up mug, they love it and want to record it for all of eternity. But for a good compromise, try to get them to agree to a "no-photos-before-10-A.M.!" rule.

• Bring your own CD player with headphones—that way you can tune everyone out if you need to, and you can avoid arguing about what kind of music everyone wants to listen to.

• Understand that there might be some moments here and there of frustration and even anger or arguing. This is pretty normal since vacations can be superstressful. "The more subjects, issues, and difficult situations that you can anticipate, the better," counsels Cookie. "There will still be confrontations, but they will be fewer in number and smaller in degree."

before she has her period!" I was sooo glad none of my friends were with us.

Tammi, 12, Kansas

My buds and I returned to my house for a snack after seeing a movie. I went into the kitchen and turned on the lights, also accidentally switching on the pool lights in the backyard. I heard one of my friends gasp, and when I turned to see what was wrong, I saw my parents skinny-dipping in the pool!

Haley, 16, Connecticut

I brought my new boyfriend over for dinner to meet my parents for the first time. My mom promised to make a special meal for him—I told her that he loved steak, so she was planning to BBQ. Unfortunately my mom totally forgot, and when my bf and I showed up for dinner, she'd made tuna noodle casserole, which was awful. Plus she was already in her pajamas because she'd had a really rough day at work.

Joy, 16, New York

We were all hanging out at my house one Saturday afternoon when my big sis showed up and started telling stories about me as a kid. One story was about how I used to love to eat dirt and one time ate a huge piece of dog poop by accident. All my friends were totally cracking up. I wanted to disappear.

Hannah, 13, Michigan

My mom and I were shopping at the local department store for new school clothes. I picked out a bunch of stuff I liked and headed for the dressing room. My mom met me a few minutes later with a pile of clothes she wanted me to try on "just for her." "I just want to see them on you," she said. (She does this all the time.) To please her, I tried on this awful sundress that had huge polka dots and flowers all over it—it looked like a little kid's Easter dress and even came with a bonnet and gloves. When I had it on, she squealed as if I was the cutest thing she'd ever seen. She made me go out to the big mirror so I could see.

I looked like I figured I would—ridiculous. Just then I spotted my crush in the mirror. I turned to hurry and get away, but my mom grabbed me to stay. I tried to quietly whisper to her that my crush was walking by. As loud as could be, she asked, "Who's walking by?" and turned just as my crush heard her and looked over at us. I thought I was going to die right there!

Anne Marie, 12, Missouri

Before our homecoming dance, I decided to let my big sister do my makeup. She was taking a really long time, and she kept saying she wanted to get it perfect. When she was finally done, I raced to the mirror to see the results. I had so much makeup on, I looked like a clown! Since I was already late, I had to just wipe off what I could and go. Everyone commented all night long on the "nice blush"!

Fern, 14, New York

EDITOR'S NOTE: GET THE LIPSTICK BRUSH AWAY FROM FERN'S SIS BEFORE SHE HURTS SOMEONE ELSE!

DEALING
WITH SIBS

As much as we love our brothers and sisters, they can definitely be a pain a lot of the time. Why do they always seem to take great pleasure in driving us crazy?

"Usually they don't mean to hurt you," says Cookie Spancer. "They're just trying to play, but sometimes it can be taken too far."

Cookie insists that an open line of communication is necessary when dealing with a sibling. Make sure they always know where they stand with you. If they cross over a line by hurtfully embarrassing or harassing you, let them know immediately. Talking can usually clear the air.

If your sibling has obviously heard you loud and clear but the behavior doesn't stop, try ignoring it. Pretend you don't even notice or leave the room. Hopefully your lack of response will make them give up.

If none of this works, consulting your parents should be the next plan. Mom or Dad could shed some light on the situation, or they may decide to have a family meeting to take care of the situation.

Chapter Five:
Fashion Faux Pas

So that copper-colored tube top and those watermel-on-hued vinyl pants that your buds said worked so well on you in the store drew some pretty terrified looks when you sported them at school. To top it off, the tube top got caught on your binder and ripped right down the center, causing you to bolt for cover in the bathroom!

Okay, maybe your fashion disaster wasn't quite as dramatic, but wait till you hear what happened to 13-year-old Tatianna in Michigan when she was show-ing off her new bathing suit! This chapter reveals some of the worst fashion disasters ever.

THE MORT-O-METER

You might want to think about keeping a coat in your locker.

Keep your coat on.

Button that coat from head to toe!

I go to a school where we have to wear uniforms. You know, the usual dark blue skirt and white blouse. I'm so used to wearing that stupid thing every day that I could get ready for school in my sleep. One morning I walked into school, met up with my friends, and took off my coat. Everyone started laughing and pointing at me. I looked down and realized I'd forgotten to put on my skirt!

Emma, 15, Maryland

EDITOR'S NOTE: ON THE RUNWAY EMMA IS DONNING THE NEW SPICE GIRLS–INSPIRED SCHOOL UNIFORM!

My best bud and I decided we were tired of our so-so style and wanted to make ourselves over. I made an appointment for us to get our hair done at my mom's salon. I went first and did my hair in this rockin' pink Farrah 'do à la Gwen Stefani. When I was done, my friend chickened out and decided not to get her hair cut at all. It was too late for me, so when

I went to school the next day, everyone kept singing "I'm Just a Girl" to me.

Beth, 15, Washington

EDITOR'S NOTE: THE PRICE WE PAY FOR BEING BEAUTIFUL!

We were on our annual family trip to the lake. We were all riding in the motorboat to fill up the gas tank. I had been swimming all day and had changed out of my bathing suit and was just wearing a towel. When we pulled the boat into the gas station, it was my job to throw the rope to the attendant. As I threw the rope, my towel fell off. The guy was so shocked, he missed the rope, and the boat just kept drifting along, with me standing there completely naked. I thought I was going to die!

Alisha, 16, Maine

I'm kind of flat, so I wear a padded bra to give me a little extra boobage. Besides my best friends, no one knew—until our school went on a camping trip. The guys raided our tent, found my bra, and strung it up on the flagpole in the center of camp for everyone to see!

Rebecca, 12, Georgia

It was homecoming my freshman year. I got this really cute short skirt, which I wore with a tube top and big platform sandals (my first time wearing them). As I was walking to the bathroom, I tripped and fell onto the concession table. Drinks spilled, cookies fell, and my skirt went up—all in front of a huge crowd! To make it worse, the DJ stopped and announced, "The concession stand is now closed."

Ely, 15, Ohio

I had just moved to a new house with my mom and younger brother. My brother was at a friend's house, and my mom was out meeting the neighbors. I took a shower, and when I got out, I realized I didn't have any clean underwear in my room. Since nobody was home, I decided to run through the house naked to the laundry room. While I was running through the

HOW TO DEAL WITH A
STYLE SLIPUP

Uh-oh. So you decided to bare that midriff *and* sport that teeny-weeny fuchsia micromini? And now it seems like everyone is talking about your, um, keen fashion sense? Well, there will probably be many more times when aliens invade your better sense and you don some crazy outfit that you wish you hadn't. But the first thing to ask yourself is: Do *you* like what you're wearing?

If you think you look pretty cool, then don't worry about what others think of your funky attire. Keep in mind that trendsetters like L'il Kim and Vitamin C probably had to endure years of negative put-downs before droves of people ended up copying their styles once they were famous.

However, if *you* decide you don't like what you're wearing, you can always throw on a jacket or change into your gym clothes. Forgot your sweats and don't have a jacket? See if one of your friends has anything you can borrow to cover up. Stuck with no alternative? Well, you're just going to have to get through the day and remain ultrapositive and confident. Or you could admit that you made a mistake and be the first person to laugh at your "accident." As long as you don't get too worked up, no one else will, either. And by the next day most people will have forgotten all about that bright orange mini.

kitchen, I slipped on one of my brother's books. I was lying on the floor in extreme pain when all of a sudden my mom, my brother, and our new neighbors walked through the door and saw me on the floor—completely nude!

Amy, 13, Illinois

I was about to go swimming with my best friend and two hot guys at a public pool. I had started to take off the shirt over my bathing suit when suddenly I could tell by the expression on the guys' faces that more than just my shirt was coming off. I had pulled my bikini top off with my shirt! Everyone at the pool saw me topless.

Lia, 15, Delaware

My friends and I bought tube tops to wear for our act in the high school talent show. During the act I was doing a cartwheel, and the snaps in the back of my top came undone and the tube top came flying off. The whole school was laughing at me. I'll never wear a tube top again!

Melissa, 14, Massachusetts

I have kind of a hard time waking up in the morning—especially in the winter, when it's still dark outside. One morning, in my usual sleepy state, I grabbed a pair of checked pants and a dark-colored tee, hurriedly dressed, and rushed off to school. When my friend saw me, she said, "Interesting outfit." I looked down and realized I'd grabbed the wrong T-shirt from the closet! I was wearing a striped shirt with checked pants! I felt like a total space cadet.

Lisa, 15, Illinois

My favorite pair of jeans had a little hole in the butt. It was pretty small, so I figured no one would notice. In fourth-period health class my bud rushed up to me. "Did you know you have a huge hole in your pants?!" I reached around—that little hole had become gigantic, and my butt was totally hanging out!

Maggie, 15, Colorado

I grabbed a pair of shorts from the laundry and slipped them on before rushing out to school. They felt kind of tight, but I thought that was because they'd just come out of the dryer. When I got to school, I heard some people laughing. I looked down and realized I'd put on my little brother's shorts, which are way too short and small for me!

Emily, 13, Texas

I put on this semibackless top and then checked myself out in the mirror. My back had a few pimples on it, so I decided not to wear the top. But then my mom suggested I should just turn it around, which I did and raced out the door. Once at school I realized how low-cut the shirt was and slipped a sweatshirt over it before too many people could see me. It was superhot, and my friends kept telling me to take off the sweatshirt. I didn't. That's the last time I listen to my mom's fashion advice!

Becky, 13, Idaho

My nails are pretty brittle, and they break all the time, so I decided to try fake ones. I got the press-on kind, put them on, and painted them a nice blue. I thought they looked pretty cool, but when my crush saw me, he was totally disgusted and said, "Why are you wearing those witch nails?" A bunch of other people were around us at the time, and they all laughed at me. But whatever—I still like them!

Sheri, 13, California

There are some major hotties in my gym class, including my crush. We were playing flag football, and a girl came running by me. She went to pull my flag off my belt, but instead she grabbed my button-up shorts. All the buttons unsnapped, and my shorts came flying off. Everybody looked at me and started cracking up.

Jeni, 13, Ohio

CLASSIC FASHION DOS AND DON'TS

Because trends are always changing and being reinvented, it's pointless to talk about specific fads. One season's major "do" can easily fall into the "don't" list in a year. But here are some style suggestions that never go out of fashion:

Don'T wear clothes that aren't your size—either way too tight or way too loose. You won't be comfortable, and the effect is never flattering.

Do wear colors that work with your skin tone, hair, and eyes. Talk to a beauty professional at a makeup counter in your favorite store if you're not sure which colors to choose.

Don'T mix and match prints. Stick to one print at a time, and pair it up with a solid basic. Accentuate by wearing one vibrantly designed piece at a time. For instance, pair a black skirt and muted top with some wild tights.

Do wear clothes that complement your figure. There are many books and magazine articles out there that can help you find the styles that suit your frame best.

My boyfriend and I went to our school's Valentine's dance. I wanted to look really hot, so I wore a tight strapless dress and these strappy heels. I had a great time, but as we were leaving, I was walking through the grass to his car, and it was all muddy. I stepped in this big pile of mud and slipped. Just as my guy caught me, I lost my balance in my funky sandals and pulled him down in the mud. To make things worse, I tore the front of my dress and had to hold it shut all the way home.

Leanna, 16, Michigan

EDITOR'S NOTE: LOOK ON THE BRIGHT SIDE. AT LEAST YOU WERE LEAVING THE DANCE!

I was riding the bus home from school. My backpack was really heavy, plus I was wearing supertall platforms. As I stepped off the bus at my stop, I completely missed the last two steps and fell to the pavement, landing on my butt. There were about fifty

FUNKIEST FASHION
FAUX PAS

I was at the prom, and we were all outside, waiting to get in. All of a sudden a burst of wind sent my dress flying up in the air. The only pair of clean underwear that I could find was my sister's Barney underwear, so that's what I was wearing! After that I was the laughingstock of the school.

KAREN, 16, OTTAWA, CANADA

people on the bus, and all of them saw me fall.

Rochelle, 13, Maine

EDITOR'S NOTE: IN THIS CASE, ROCHELLE MIGHT WANT TO THINK ABOUT KEEPING ANOTHER PAIR OF SHOES IN HER LOCKER! REMEMBER, PEOPLE: A HEAVY BACKPACK AND PLATFORMS NEVER GO TOGETHER.

I had to go in front of the entire student body to receive an award at school. I bought a really short skirt and high heels for the occasion. When I was walking up the stairs to get my award, the back of my heel broke, and I fell forward. My skirt went up, and everyone saw my red lacy underwear. I ran off the stage, limping because I only had one heel. I was mortified!

Samantha, 17, New York

One Friday night my friends and I headed to a dance club. We got really dressed up and wore tube tops and miniskirts. I'm really flat-chested, so I put toilet paper in my bra. Once we were at the club, I started dancing with this hot guy and accidentally bumped into a girl carrying a drink. The soda spilled over my chest and soaked the toilet paper, totally deflating my "chest." I've never been so embarrassed!

Deena, 12, Colorado

I was in swimming class, and I had just bought a new bathing suit. When I got out of the pool to show my friends my new suit, all the guys stopped swimming and stared at me, and all the girls just kept laughing. Finally one of my friends came up to me and said, "I like your suit, but did you know that it's see-through?" My face turned red, and I ran out of the pool area. After a year I still get teased about it.

Tatianna, 13, Michigan

One day before a basketball game, three other cheerleaders were holding me up for a stunt. While I was up in the air, the pad in my bra slipped out of my shirt and fell onto the ground. The cheerleaders burst out laughing and dropped me. I thought I would be clever, so I said, "Whoops, my shoulder pad fell out." Then I stuck the pad into my uniform like a real shoulder pad. Obviously that didn't work because it just made them laugh even harder.

Jennifer, 15, Alabama

I was so excited when my crush invited me to a Britney Spears concert. I wanted to impress him, so I wore a supercute, supertight tube top. At the concert I started jumping up and down and dancing to a fast song, not realizing that my boob had popped out of my shirt. I sat down after the song ended, and my crush said, "Um, you might want to tuck that back in." How embarrassing!

Carrie, 14, Kentucky

I wanted to surprise all my friends and especially my boyfriend by getting a new look, so I made an appointment for a haircut. I got crazy and went really short. I guess the hairdresser was new because she completely messed up my hair and ended up having to practically shave it off. My hair was way shorter than I had wanted it. My boyfriend now calls me "Baldy."

Sidney, aka Baldy, 16, Indiana

EDITOR'S NOTE: SIDNEY MIGHT WANT A HAT, TOO!

I n class one day I was reapplying my lipstick (without a mirror since I'm so used to doing it) when my friend gave me this really weird look. I pulled out my compact and realized that I had just smeared cover-up all over my lips. I didn't have any tissue paper, so I had to wait until class was over to run to the bathroom and wipe off my lips.

Ericka, 17, New Jersey

THINGS TO KEEP IN YOUR LOCKER IN CASE OF A FASHION EMERGENCY

1. An extra pair of casual pants, like sweats or jeans.

2. A sweatshirt—to tie around your waist if your skirt is too short, or something ripped, or you're chilly.

3. Flip-flops or tennies—to change into before third period, after the pain caused by those boots you just had to have becomes unbearable.

4. A sweater you can throw on to cover up a disaster.

5. If you have to wear a uniform, a clean shirt—in case you spill on yourself.

6. A bandanna or a hat to cover up bad hair—or bobby pins, rubber bands, barrettes, etc.

*Okay, so you can't fit everything in there, but one or two items should rescue you!

—*From Andrea D'Angelo, owner of superhip Trio,*
an Encino, California, clothing store

Chapter Six:
Bod Clods

With all its different parts and private "functions," your body practically offers a smorgasbord of potential humiliation. But it goes with being human, so you're really not alone!

Fifteen-year-old Susannah from Arizona faced an awkward shock when she decided to sport a new, oh-so-clingy dress to her school dance. You'll read all about her smooth moves on the dance floor and how she—and everyone else in this chapter—dealt with these tricky dilemmas.

THE MORT-O-METER

Barely Blew It

Way Blew It

Totally blew it—
time to join the circus!

I was in algebra, the last period of the day, and I was really tired because I had stayed up late the night before. I ended up falling asleep in class, and I only woke up when I heard my teacher call my name. The whole class was cracking up. I looked down and saw that I had drooled all over my desk. To make matters worse, I was sitting next to the cutest guy in school. He was so disgusted that he raised his hand and asked if he could move to another seat.

Cara, 13, Massachusetts

I was at this really cool shoe store, shopping for new shoes. It was kind of a hot day, so I was wearing sneakers with no socks. I picked out a couple of pairs of sandals and asked the salesclerk if I could try them on, then sat down and started to take off my shoes. There was this really cute guy trying on some Sketcher shoes just a few seats down from me who was checking me out. I smiled and slipped off my shoes. That's when I just about fell over—my feet were horrendously stinky! I looked up at the cute guy to see if he had noticed. He was holding his nose and grimacing. Then he got up and quickly left the store.

Tamara, 15, Texas

EDITOR'S NOTE: TWO WORDS: ODOR EATERS.

On my first date with this guy I'd been crushing on for months, I let out a "silent but deadly" fart. There was no one else to pin the blame on, but I still looked around, pretending to be searching for a culprit. Later my guilt got the best of me, so while we were talking on the phone the next day, I blurted out that it had been me who farted. He laughed and said he'd had a stuffed-up nose and hadn't even been able to smell anything. He'd never have known if I hadn't said anything!

Val, 16, Washington

I bought this beautiful dress for the prom. I'm a little flat-chested, though, so I wore those inserts that make your boobs look and feel bigger. I started to dance to this fast song, and I smacked my arm into the prom queen's chest while she was walking by. She got really mad and said, "You know, some of our boobs are real." Then she pointed down to the floor and started laughing. I looked in horror to see that one of my inserts had fallen out while I was dancing!

Jamie, 18, Illinois

went to spend the day at this campground with my aunt, her friend, and her friend's really hot son. We decided to go swimming, so the guy and I jumped in together. When I came up, my aunt kept saying my name as she rubbed under her nose. It took me a minute until I realized she was trying to signal to me that I had snot hanging from my nose. I wiped it and thought the guy hadn't noticed that it was there, but he started laughing and said, "Yeah, I noticed that, too, but I didn't want to point it out and embarrass you!"

Cameron, 13, Illinois

y boyfriend and I were at his grandmother's

house when I started my period, and all I could find were Depends, those diapers for old people. I didn't want to stuff toilet paper in my pants, so I put on one of the diapers, thinking that no one would notice. Later that evening we decided to watch TV with some of his relatives. I was sitting on my boyfriend's lap, and he must have felt something squishy because he yelled, "Are you wearing diapers?!" I was completely mortified.

Stella, 15, Canada

I invited my crush over to watch TV. We were sitting on the couch and had started kissing when I suddenly had the urge to sneeze. When I did, a huge glob of snot flew out of my nose and landed on his shirt. He gave me a strange look, then said, "You are a very interesting girl!" and quickly left. That was my worst date ever!

Jasmine, 14, Florida

EDITOR'S NOTE: SOUNDS LIKE JASMINE'S GUY WAS A REAL SNOT!

At our school dance I was having a great time. I knew I looked hot in my new dress, and I'm a pretty good dancer, too. When my absolute favorite song came on, I got way into it, spinning around, clapping, doing MTV dance contest stuff. I guess I got a little too enthusiastic because the next thing I knew, one of my boobs popped out of my dress and hit the cute guy dancing next to me in the face!

Susannah, 15, Arizona

I was at my boyfriend's house for my fifteenth birthday. He took my hand and led me down to the basement. We started kissing, and suddenly the overhead light flickered on and all my friends jumped out and yelled, "Surprise!" He and I tried to pull away, but our braces hooked together—we were stuck! Everyone started to laugh hysterically, and we couldn't get unhooked. We had to walk sideways up the stairs where both his and my parents were and plead for them to unhook us. They finally did—once they were done laughing.

Courtney, 15, Pennsylvania

EDITOR'S NOTE: THE GOOD THING ABOUT THIS ONE IS THAT COURTNEY AND HER BF WERE ABLE TO SHARE THE PAIN!

I wore a strapless dress to prom. Since I don't have a strapless bra, I decided to go without one. I was named prom queen, and when we were dancing, my klutzy king stepped on my long dress. Out popped my boobs!

Veronica, 17, Texas

My cousin and I went to the mall. I had a really bad runny nose, so she told me to rip off a little piece of tissue paper and stuff it in my nostril. I did, and she said it wasn't noticeable. Everything was fine until we started talking to some hotties at the food court. One of them said, "You have a white string in your nose," and pulled on it. Out came the tissue and snot flung all over him! He was totally grossed out.

J. T., 13, Maryland

EDITOR'S NOTE: WHY WAS HE TUGGING ON SOME-
THING COMING OUT OF HER NOSE, ANYWAY? IT
DOESN'T SOUND LIKE J. T. IS MISSING OUT ON
MUCH!

I needed a new look for prom, so I tried a red hair rinse. It looked great, and I was psyched to show it off. At the prom my friends and I were dancing and having a really good time. I was moving around a lot and started to sweat. I noticed a lot of people staring at me, and one of my friends told me to check my face. When I got out my mirror, I saw reddish streaks running down the side of my face and neck!

Jen, 15, Minnesota

Our track coach was having us train for a marathon. During one of the long-distance runs my stomach started to feel really upset. I was at least four miles from the nearest bathroom, so I picked up my pace to try to get there faster. I was able to hold out for about three miles, but in the fourth mile I couldn't wait any longer and ended up pooping in my sweats. It was so gross.

Francie, 16, California

My crush was sitting behind me in computer class. I was wearing my brand-new, white capri pants. I heard him laughing and whispering, so I turned around to see what was so funny. On his computer screen in bold red letters it said, "Cathy's got her period!" I turned around, totally embarrassed, and saw a bloodstain on my pants. I wanted to cry!

Cathy, 13, Montana

I've always been a tomboy. But in seventh grade I started to develop this huge chest. I tried to pretend they weren't there, so I didn't even wear a bra. During an after-school softball game, with most of the school watching, I hit an amazing home run. As I was charging into home, I heard this guy yell, "Get a bra!" I was mortified and made my mom take me bra shopping immediately after the game was over.

Hilary, 14, California

EDITOR'S NOTE: THE GUY WHO YELLED AT HILARY SHOULD BE EMBARRASSED FOR BEING A TOTAL JERK!

PASS THAT PAD! HOW TO PERIOD-PROOF YOURSELF FROM MONTHLY ACCIDENTS

Yikes! It seems like you're always having some kind of menstruation mishap! Here are some ways to minimize period probs:

• **CHANGE YOUR PAD OR TAMPON REGULARLY.** Okay, so this one has already been drilled into your brain by Mom, the school nurse, and even the back of the Tampax box, but it can still be easy to forget. You get caught up in something and think, I'll just keep it in there an extra hour. Wrong answer! Not only are you less likely to have accidents if you change your tampons often, but it's much safer and healthier, too.

• **ALWAYS KEEP A FEW EXTRA PADS OR TAMPONS IN YOUR BACKPACK AND YOUR LOCKER.** That way you'll be sure to have protection when you need it, wherever you happen to be at the time.

- **K**EEP A SWEATSHIRT HANDY. It's very useful to wrap around your waist in case of any leakage.

- **H**AVE AN EXTRA PAIR OF JEANS AROUND. This one might not always be possible, but if it is—it's a great idea. That way you can change if there's a serious staining problem.

- **W**EAR DARK COLORS. You always hear stories about girls getting big stains on their *white* pants. So learn the lesson—*don't wear* white pants that week! Stick to dark colors and thicker material like denim, which offers more of a buffer. So if you do have an accident, it will be less likely to show.

My crush and I were making out at a party when we split apart and he said, "Yuck!" and grabbed a tissue from a nearby box. He handed it to me and said, "That pimple on your forehead just popped." I was mortified!

Lupe, 14, California

I have Spanish right after gym. One day I walked into class, and the room smelled like really bad BO. The guy behind me sniffed the air and waved his hand in front of his face. Then the girl next to me pointed at me, like I was the one. Horrified, I leaned down to sniff my pits—and sure enough, it was me! I'd forgotten to put deodorant on after playing basketball.

Deanna, 14, Ohio

During the summer I spend most of my days at

BIGGEST
BOD BUNGLE

I was on a date with my boyfriend. We had just finished having dinner, and I had to go to the bathroom. I went in the stall and did my thing. When I came out, my boyfriend put his arm around me and then pulled back in disgust. "Ew, what's all over you?" he yelled. Everyone in the restaurant looked up. I had poop all over the bottom of my shirt! I guess I hadn't held it away from the toilet. I couldn't wait to get home!

RACHEL, 16, RHODE ISLAND

the club my family belongs to, taking tennis classes. The pool and snack bar are on the ground level, and to get to the tennis courts, you have to go down a steep set of stairs from the pool. One afternoon our tennis class was taking a water break on the pool level. When it was time to return to the courts, we all headed down the stairs. The girl behind me said something really rude about a girl in the pool (who I knew and liked from school). I spun around and chewed her out, really letting her have it. I turned back around, feeling satisfied that I had told her off, but I guess I turned around too fast because I lost my balance and ended up falling down the whole flight of stairs. Everyone was laughing at me—especially the mean girl!

Belle, 16, Florida

In English one time I raised my hand to answer a question. When the teacher called on me, I opened my mouth to speak but belched instead. The whole class laughed. My teacher said, "Correct answer!" I was totally embarrassed.

Elissa, 15, New York

We were on a family road trip, and my brother, my sister, and I had each brought a friend along. It was really hot, and we were drinking tons of water and soda. I had to pee so badly, I thought I was going to burst. We were two miles from a rest stop, and my dad was trying to make it there as fast as he could. Then my brother said something really funny. I totally cracked up and peed all over myself. The worst part was that I'd had a crush on my brother's friend for years, and now he can't even look me in the eye anymore!

Sara, 16, Utah

How to Minimize Looking
Like a Bod Clod

According to University of California, Los Angeles, education professor Linda Sax, every once in a while your body might do something that embarrasses you in public. For instance, you might get your period unexpectedly (while wearing white shorts), you might have a glob of snot hanging from your nose (while talking to a cute guy), or you might accidentally make a loud burp (while having dinner at a friend's house). The most important thing to remember is that these things happen to everyone. We just wish that they only happened to us in private! But if your body decides to betray you in public, here are a few things Linda suggests you should do.

STEP 1: DON'T OVERREACT. You might find that nobody else actually noticed what happened. If it's obvious that others *have* noticed, then move on to step 2.

STEP 2: CONSIDER YOUR AUDIENCE. If you're with your friends, then the best thing to do is laugh the whole thing off. If you don't make a big deal out of it, chances are

they won't, either. Get them to laugh *with* you, not *at* you. However, if you're in a more formal setting, just excuse yourself politely and go take care of business (getting a pad or tampon, wiping your nose, etc.). Again, the incident will probably be quickly forgotten.

STEP 3: *MOVE ON!* These embarrassing moments happen to everyone at one time or another. You can even use them as learning experiences so that next time something potentially humiliating happens, you're prepared to deal with it quickly and smoothly.

I was making out with my boyfriend when he went to kiss my ears. All of a sudden he stopped and spit. I asked him what was wrong. He pulled away from me and said, "Waxy buildup. You should use Q-tips!" I turned bright red.

Melissa, 15, Nevada

I play a lot of tennis and end up losing my toenails a lot—they get really rank from being in sweaty tennis shoes for hours on end and usually end up getting infected and falling off. Anyway, during one of my tennis matches once, I twisted my ankle. My mom took me to the doctor, who was the cutest, youngest-looking doctor I'd ever seen. When he went to examine my ankle, his hand slid across my toes, pulling off a couple of toenails. He jumped away at first, thinking he'd hurt me. I was as grossed out as he was.

Ruthie, 16, Tennessee

THINGS TO KEEP IN YOUR LOCKER IN CASE OF A BOD CRISIS

If there's any room left after you've filled your locker with items to prevent suffering a fashion faux pas, you may want to stuff some of these in there as well:

- *TAMPONS AND/OR PADS*
- *TISSUES*
- *ASPIRIN*
- *ANTACIDS*
- *BREATH MINTS OR GUM*
- *CLEAN UNDIES, IN CASE OF ANY ACCIDENTS*
- *COVER-UP*
- *A MIRROR*

Just a couple of these items stashed in your locker or back-pack could save you some big-time humiliation!

CONCLUSION

By now you definitely know you're not alone when it comes to looking like a dork in front of your crush or getting caught in a mortifying situation at school. Tons of other girls (and guys!) just like you have been through their own horrifying experiences. And you've got to admit, a lot of them are pretty hilarious.

And if you can laugh at this collection of catastrophes, hopefully you feel at least a little better about *your* embarrassing moments. The most important thing is to always be willing to laugh at yourself first. That way no one will be laughing *at* you; they'll just be laughing *with* you!